Letters To My Dead Parents

Dani Marie

BookLeaf Publishing

India | USA | UK

Made with ❤ on the BookLeaf Publishing Platform
www.bookleafpub.in
www.bookleafpub.com

Dedication

To those living and beyond, who taught me how to love
the world, one another, and of course myself.

Preface

The idea of death is something that has followed me through my life. I have had more people die than most would consider normal at 26 years. The biggest being my parents, my dad in 2019 and my mom in 2023. There is never enough time, nor a proper way to grieve. These poems show my grief throughout the years, as well as my slow crawl toward coping. In the end I express how I have been able to find a love that has helped me find the beauty in the world.

My hope is that someone can read these poems who is grieving and realize that they are not alone.

Acknowledgements

I want to thank all the people who have stayed with me through every grief, heartbreak, and break down. To my family who remind me of my worth, and even when I can't, they make me laugh and remember good times. A special thanks to the family members who have taken on the role of parental figures whenever I needed guidance. To Diana, for helping me with my art work for the cover, and for always being there to answer my phone calls no matter the time of day. To Amaris, for always reminding me to keep writing, and that my voice matters. Thank you to Jack, Maya, Larry, Alli and Ismari, for believing in me and hyping me up always. To grandma, thank you for staying with me at my mothers death bed, even in your walker and days before your surgery. To every high school English teacher that encouraged me. To my cocker spaniel Kylo, who will always be my little prince, thank you for jumping with joy when I come home even after a tough day, and for cuddling me when I'm sick. I love each and every one of you.

Of course with such adoration and love, to Adrian. There is no amount of poems I could write to tell you how thankful, or how in love I am. I never imagined I would have someone who truly gets me, and makes me feel like my parents would be happy I have you.

Intro: The Question

What is it like to live with depression?

A question it seems;

I get far too often;

No I am not bothered by it;

Rather confused they think I have some regime.

Because I thought by now I'd be in a coffin.

So instead I help

And try to pretend I can explain;

What is it like to live with depression?

Part One: The Discovery

The strum of the guitar is suddenly dull and bland.

Hanging out with friends she feels like a fish on dry
land;

You can't breath and you are trying to furiously get out
of the sand.

But she did belong there once with such high command.

But I guess life can't always be so grand.

Still weeks later she still feels like she's on quicksand.

She wants to know why she does not recognize her own
hand;

Her own body she wishes to disband.

She tried to hang in there, after all life isn't always
planned.

Still she feels like she can no longer stand

There is no happiness for her and she cannot understand.

She screams trying to piece together any strand;

Then she realizes,

"Oh shit, I am depressed."

Death my beloved
Pre Mom, Post Dad

It is lent season and I am supposed to give up something
for 40 days and nights.
I'm supposed to give up something that is a pleasure in
my life.
Deciding what to give up is a useless fight.
For me there is nothing so pleasing in my life.

Giving up social media is something I don't care for for
long.
It doesn't do anything except keep me busy when
depressed.
Maybe I should give up song.
Then again I don't think I'm supposed to give up
something that will make me depressed

If I wanted to really give up something to benefit
I would give up the hate and disgust I have for myself.
I would stop treating myself like some anti feminist.
I would give up the inconsolable loath I have for myself

Because then,

" I shall 'worship' thee body and soul that God hath

given me. I shall fill thy body with love and peace. No longer will this body be thine enemy, but thy gift from the heavens."

But I am not as religious as my family would desire.
I do not remember what it is like to love yourself.
Giving up how much I hate the creation of god that is myself is now dire.
Instead I look in the mirror and say, "You should be repelled by yourself."

I am not Satan's tool
I am death's
I am my own fool
I wallow and baptize myself in the whispers of death

I am someone the bible does not recognize
I belong to a special kind of hell the bible that does not have knowledge
One that satan has not seen with his own eyes
Because I built it with my own knowledge

For lent I will give up lying to myself.
I will understand what I am
No longer will I put conviction on a shelf
I will understand who I am

Because then,

" I shall 'persecute' thee body and soul that God hath
given me. I shall fill thy body with death and
taciturnity. No longer will this body be thine savior, but
thy dirge from the unknown hell"
 I am floating in a purgatory I created
Maybe that is why death follows me around
Because he too lies here ill fated
Trying to figure out where we will exist when our time
is no longer around

Only i can decide if heaven or hell will claim my soul
My free will is what peaks death's interest.
I will not dedicate myself to worship or persecution to
feel whole
Instead I will spend my days discovering my best interest

Because then,

"I shall 'sustain' thee body and soul that God hath given
me. I shall fill thy body with knowledge and curiosity.
No longer will this body be thine doubt, but thy
receptacle for purgatory"

Breaking News: Depression is in.

A popular notion it seems I have fallen victim.
The idea that I hate who I am; who I have become.
I cannot believe that such a calamity, I would succumb.
But since I was age 13 I remember such feelings.

How I wish I could wash away the resentment for my
body
Like I wash away all the dirt on me after a tiresome day
of existence.
But the kind of dread I felt it returns with such
persistence.
It is not situation induced, for me it is a birth gift.

My mother, with all her desire, wished it was teenage
angst.
Something solvable with time, that age would cause
withdraw.
That my emotions were simply on a see-saw.
To her disappointment years later I can tell you she was
wrong.

Part Two: The Fight

8

She had no fight with Depression, it filled her and consumed her, and brought all its friends to watch the fall.

Part Three: The Fall

No matter the situation she is filled with Anger at all time.

The reason why, well there is no more denying;

It is Depression's underrated partner in crime.

Anger, it fills her lungs and leaves her prying,

For she is now looking in the mirror and lying.

She says that the anger is normal and can be justified

But for this type of pain there is no applying;

It is a nightmare that is heavily allied.

Depression makes her furious even in her prime.

Every little thing in her life has now become terrifying;

For she can no longer enjoy her lifetime;

She is now bound to Depression's lies, forever complying,

Even toward her former loves, there is no defying.

So Anger pulls her along with a quick snide,

As Depression looks on applauding Anger, forever gratifying,

No matter how hard she screamed and cried.

A friend sings out with a chime,

Depression and Anger tells her it is the worst sound, so horrifying,

So she no longer finds solace in any rhyme;

All because her demons told her and now it makes her Angry, without verifying.

Her heart, Depression and Anger are forever occupying

They kick back on the couch simply along for the ride.

They petty remarks she is always buying.

What's the point of trying if they took your pride?

Death: Revisited

Post Mom, Post Dad

The bible recognizes death as the result of sin.
It is something or someone that is feared from all
From different cultures and ethnicities.
I however recognize him as someone so akin

Death tears at the seams of my memories and dreams.
I am on a leash so tight, with no end in sight.

Though I try to claw my way out from Death's hold,
I am helpless in the face of something so malevolent.
All I can do is watch, as the ones around me.
To Death they are sold.

Myself I begin to blame as if Death I became.
As I rip off my clothes, in the mirror I see Death's oaths.

Out of breath and confused,
Am I Deaths unwilling partner in crime?
Did he find my faith so delectable and inviting?
So toward my loves did he misuse.

Mother, father I am so guilt ridden, if I am the one that is
unbidden.

If only I could end this family curse, for Death to finally
disperse

But I will not turn the tides on my own heart.
For that would be a forfeit of battle I intend to win.
I will not give Death the satisfaction of seeing my
defeat.
I will do everything to keep my loves and Death apart.

In Death's arms I will not find solace in something so
lawless.
Until we meet again, I will talk to you with my pen.

The Past 10 Years

It has been 10 years since I saw my grandmother in a coffin
It has been 6 years since I saw my uncle in a coffin
It has been 5 years since I saw my father in a coffin
It has been 3 years since I saw my cousin in a coffin
It has been 2 years since I saw my mother in a coffin
It has been 1 year since I saw my great grandmother in a coffin.

It has been 2 minutes since I wondered where I would be if those coffins were never filled.

It has been 1 minute since I cried with grief.

Part Four: The Death

She screams into the void;

Piercingly and endlessly with pain.

Her presence they wish to avoid;

But what could one possibly gain;

From ignoring what could be death;

Except inexplicable guilt;

When she takes her own breath;

And the body begins to wilt.

Dear Dad

The ones you knew who loved me, they don't love me
like they used to.
The one who used to hurt me, I haven't seen him in
years.
But I got a few who stuck around, I got some news ones
that make me feel like I'm worth it.
The one that I love now, well he takes away all of the
doubt.
I wish you could know him now, wish you could shake
his hand, wish that you knew his name.

Because, the world keeps turning while I'm still
mourning.
I keep on loving, even if it hurts me.
I know you wouldn't want to see me sad.
Been five years since the last I love you's were said.
Hope heaven is as good as they said.

I know mom's gone to see you, hope she told you how
I've grown up.
And the house you two left me, I still walk through with
all these memories.
I got these new hobbies now, new things that make up
who I am.

And the life that I live now, well it's different than I imagined.

I wish you could know me now, wish you could see me love, wish you could hold me tight.

Dear Mom

I wish I could say I am not angry. I wish I could say I found solace in your death like I did dad's. I wish I could say there was absolutely no resentment, and only love, and memories. But that is not true.

As my last living parent I expected you to be there until I was older. I expected you to be able to see me walk down the aisle. I expected you to see me birth a child. I expected you to tell me you were proud of what I had become in my middle ages. But that is not true.

Instead I am ridden with confusion and distaste when I see photos of what was, or when I hear stories of those who still have their family together. I am jealous of something so simple, that they or I have no control over.

So I wonder, when will I no longer resent you. When will I no longer see your death as the tipping point to loneliness. When will I no longer believe that I am unworthy of a family.

But god do I still love you, and I know you left me with so much for me to love, that you loved as well. I know that you loved the house you left me, with such fond

times. I know that you loved the dog you left me that
greets me every time I get home, and lays on the bed
with me when I am ill. I know that you loved the family
you left me that calls me and checks up on me. I know
you loved my friends that called you.

But at this moment, I know that you also loved the boy
you got to meet, who took my heart.

If there is ever anything I am thankful for not because of,
but in despite of, your passing, is that you got to meet
the one I love.

I told you on your deathbed, and I will tell you again in
writing, don't worry about me. He'll take care of me. The
family will take care of me. The friends will take care of
me. The dog will take care of me. And I know
somewhere along the lines I'll turn that resentment into
thankfulness, and that feeling of unworthiness into love.

One day I will love you the way you always wanted.

Bowling Night.

I am angry at people who don't even know it
I am angry at the people who believed all would be fine
I am angry in honor of people who have guided me
I am angry for the person who loved me when I could
not
I am angry for my city
For the state
For the country
For the world.

God, I am just so angry.

Anyway, time to smile.
It's my turn to bowl.
Can't let them know.

I'm seething with anger.

Time

Time does not feel straightforward
Every time I believe I am no longer sad, I look back not
forward
And even when I feel like something pushes me forward
I am stuck in a cavern with stairs up back, and a wall
forward.

My emotions sway like an incoherent seesaw with no
way off.
And I revisit events that I thought I had brushed off.
Only to find out that any self reflection is turned off.
Every death makes me feel like my world is off.

What I solved with my father comes back when there's a
new one.
So when I lost my mother, again I believed death was my
only one.
Fighting tirelessly to win death's one on one.
Because in the end left standing, there could be just one.

Sandbox

I miss my sandbox.

I miss digging my chubby little 6-year-old fingers into the sand and burying rocks with my friends that we said were friendship rocks.

I miss squishing my feet in the sand and watching the people in the swings in front of me.

I miss hearing the whistle of the teacher telling us it was time to get back into the school.

I miss bringing my white cat stuffed animal to school and making up songs for it.

I miss swinging on that stupid swing set with its stupid sand.

Because it is no longer sand. It's wood chips.

Hard, sharp wood chips that pierce my 18-year-old feet when I tried to use the swing.

My long fingers grip the chains of the swing so hard it's like I can already feel the imprint it will leave.

I hate the wood chips that I have to dig my feet into to start swinging.

I hate that I can't tell if my friendship rock is below the stupid wood chips.

Where's my sandbox?

I miss my sandbox.

I can feel the wind picking up and slapping my hair
across my face,
occasionally wiping away the tears that fall down my
cheek.
I wanted to stay there forever and just keep swinging.
Maybe I'd swing so high I'd fly into space and never have
to deal with wood chips ever again.
I miss my sandbox.

Sadly, I need to stop swinging.
I need to dig my feet in the wood chips to stop myself,
because I have a friend I need to go visit.
One that I probably buried a friendship rock with.
I hope he hates wood chips too.

I don't want to go back to my friend's house,
because for the hundredth time I have to pretend I'm
okay.
I have to pretend like I don't hate these stupid wood
chips.
I have to pretend like I didn't despise the bundt cake I
bought earlier
because I had to scarf it down to get out of my house as
fast as I could;
In order to make it to this park,

with these stupid wood chips.

The swing next to me is empty I notice
and I don't want it to be.
 I never want it to be.

 I didn't want it to be empty when I got out of the car
with tears in my eyes.
I didn't want it to be empty when I said I needed to go
take a walk.
I wanted someone to fill the swing and hate the wood
chips as much as I do.
And to miss the sandbox.
I REALLY miss the sandbox.

It is at this moment that I realize something.
You.
The one I wanted to fill the swing because you were the
only one around that knew I was there crying.
You.
The one who waited in the car because you thought I'd
be better off alone,
when I've never liked being alone when I'm sad.
You.
The one who couldn't seem to understand that when I
am alone I fall into the dark place.
You.

You are my wood chips.

The ones I dig my feet into even though I hate it so damn
much.
The one I keep on dealing with just because I get to feel
the adrenaline of the swing set,
even though in order to start and end the swing, I have
to pierce myself with the wood chips

You are the wood chips, and I am still screaming out that
I miss my sandbox.
Where in the hell is my sandbox?
And I realize the sandbox will never grow here again.

So to save myself I need to leave the swing set with the
stupid wood chips behind,
and find my new sandbox,
One that will caress my feet softly and sweetly,
and one that will let me bury my friendship rock in.

Dear Madison

At least I had common sense to try
To try and communicate with you
Before you decided I was not enough
Before you left with everyone I loved

If I wasn't supposed to be perfect
Why did you scream when I spilled water
If i wasn't supposed to be like a dream
Why did you cry when you woke up

I still love you
I hope you know
I think you can feel it
Because I still long for your attention

I let you hurt me over and over again
Over and over
Over and over.
Again. Again

I don't care though.
If you are the shark that ends me
At least I'll get to see my favorite animal
Before I succumb completely.

So stay with me
So I can dream just a little better
So waste my time
So I can breathe a little longer

Don't leave me again okay?
I let you break me apart
Until I remade myself
Into something you were okay with.

So don't leave me.
I broke the veins that pumped my blood
Until the only things that ran through me
Was your breath

If only I could take away every thorn
from every rose bush,
so you could own every rose.

The Artist

I am an artist paint red roses
Purple and yellow tulips too
All by hand on my
Perfectly crooked canvas

But I don't wanna be artist no more
I don't wanna paint anything else
Cause I don't wanna feel this pain
Not again.

I don't wanna sketch the vines that bind me
To the bed where I can't see past
Can't see past tomorrow no more
Can't see past anything else

My body is my perfectly crooked canvas
Am I finally pretty enough
Am I finally good enough
Am I finally colorful enough

For me.

Part Six: Lovers Revival

Dreaming of loves true kiss
Imaging it as first as some dark gothic romance
Something my teenage heart believed was the epitome of
perfection
But loves revival came in the form of something different

It came in the form of awkward first dates.
Scared to touch hands at first.
First kiss that came with consent
Which in turn was more alluring than I realized

At that moment my heart understood,
It was not a mysterious person
Who would treat me like a possession, And change who
I was
That I truly wanted.

Instead what I wanted,
And needed,
Was the boy in front of me
So wonderfully open minded.

Who was willing to listen to my tethered heart,
Who was willing to ask what I needed

Who was willing to treat memories of my dead parents
as a cure
Instead of a plague

Loves revival came, early August,
Whilst my mother was still breathing,
To help prepare me for when she wasn't
And remind me, I am still my parents' daughter.

Looking Forward

The day that I met him I was trying to prove a point.
I believed that I was unlikable and unlovable, and I
needed that to change.
Trying to rope someone into my delusions may make me
seem derange.
But the system I thought I had, had fallen apart in the
palm of my hands.

You see I look at myself and only see adjectives of pain
I see fat body, big feet, gross lips, nothing for anyone to
gain
yet in me I also see my eyes and it brings me pain
for I see the eyes of my father that I gain

So instead I gave it my best shot to fall in love.
And fall in love did I, so fast in a whirlwind
All of my fears have suddenly thinned.
I am now discovering love, of all kind

The first time his name left my lips,
It shivered through my body,
As if each cell had to whisper it from its lips
To make sure he was embedded in every part of my body

I was enamored in ways I did not know,
My heart and soul deserved.
Every good part of me he preserved
Until I could fully admit I was in love

I'm not the daughter of a martyr
But I sure as hell would die for this.
Not for the title of martyr
But to secure in my life to have this.

I will mend all my bridges
Just to let him have the best me
In love and carefree
Nothing but looking forward

For the first time I will look forward
Even if the path is dark,
I know he will help light the spark
To move on from my past

Dear Mom and Dad

I think you'd be ecstatic to know I've found love. True love. I believe with all my soul it is true love. I also believe it without a doubt because I refuse to believe the universe would take you both away from me and at least not give me someone in compensation. Don't get me wrong your lives are not something I would gamble to feel a lover's embrace, but if he is what I am gifted for the years of yearning you both, then I believe I will be okay.

In him I have found comfort like no other. When my support system left me, he was the one who reminded me I am still worthy. He is the one who let me cry in the shower. Who knows when I'm breaking down I repeat certain words over and over like I am trying to get everyone around me to believe it. But he doesn't believe the horrible things I say about myself. Instead he holds me and cries with me. Dad, can you believe I found someone so secure about his emotions he cries with me! I remember how vulnerable you were with me also. Thank you for crying in the car with me and showing me it was okay.

He also knows how to help out, and kill the cockroaches

in the room, even if he hates them too. He takes out the trash for me when it's too late and cold outside, and he'll drive me anywhere I want so I don't have to drive. Mom, can you believe I found someone so protective of me who never yells at me, and instead listens and learns.

The family loves him. They make him laugh, and he makes them laugh. We're talking about marriage. He let me pick out a ring. We're engaged. Mom, I found your wedding dress. Can I wear it? Dad, I found your boutonnieres. Can he use it?

Mom, my tia wants to take me dress shopping. Will you watch over me? Dad, my brothers want to walk me down the aisle. Will you still be there next to us?

Can we dance to your guys first dance song? Can I use the same pillows for the rings you guys had? Can I replicate your wedding? Like you're still here. Like you're with me. Like I'm still close to you. Please. I'm begging.

Grief

Grief is a complex thing.
It is not sexist, or homophobic, or racist,
it does not care if you have just met up with it a couple
of years ago.
It has no restrictions

I have been told that love replicated grief.
That the harder you love,
the harder you grief,
and it is just proof of love

I learned to love from my parents
With every fiber of my being
Tearing myself apart so loves strength shines
Consuming everything that I am

Even if it hurts

I guess that means I grief the same
With every fiber of my being
Tearing myself apart so grief's strength shines
Consuming everything that I am

Even if it hurts

I wish they'd taught me something important
Like how to do taxes
Like how to have a cleaning schedule
Like how to not cry when dusting off their urns.

A reflection of caring for them while alive.
The wash cloth I'd lovingly clean their face with
Is now used to pick up dirt and tears
and is now a form of grief.

I wish they didn't teach me how to love.
Fully and unapologetically

But I need to give way for love
The same way I am allowing grief
To consume all of me.
Love has that same capability.

Love is a complex thing.
It is not sexist, or homophobic, or racist,
it does not care if you have just met up with it a couple
of years ago.
It has no restrictions

In their urns I will see the reflection of love
I will see myself get older

Married, and wiser
Completing goals consumed by love

I am glad they taught me how to love.
Fully and unapologetically.

Morning Coffee

On a Saturday morning we're up early,
Getting ready for a date at the zoo.
I go to the kitchen to make a cup of coffee,
When suddenly I have a breakthrough.

My mother's words echo throughout my mind.
She missed having morning coffee with my father.
In the morning she'd cry into her cup
For the things she once loved are now a bother.

It was a sentiment I could not entirely grasp.
Loving someone so much they change your daily drink.
Suddenly coffee was so much more to her than a way to
stay awake
 It was her hearts way of finding a link.

Her and my father were connected by a morning cup
That filled her life and her heart
 In his absence the drink is now bland
Every morning she wishes to restart

That bond, that commitment, that love, that care
I finally understand.

I see the change in my caffeinated drink
It is sweeter and more smooth.
In it I see your reflection.
It gives me answers to help soothe.

It is the silkiness of your arms around me.
The way you warm me up on cold winter nights.
The calm of your voice when I am stressed.
The bold taste of you showing me new sights.

You are everything that brings me peace
and helps start my day
Whether we are home alone
or in a brand new cafe

Every morning I want with you.
Every grief I want with you
Every questioning of the future I want with you
Every new friend, job, hobby, I want with you.

So I'll hand you the morning coffee
as we head to the zoo
you'll drive as we sip our drinks
and I'll tell you about my new breakthrough

9 789369 540761